WORLD SOCCER LEGENDS

WOMEN'S WORLD CUP 2019

Abbeville Press Publishers
New York · London

A portion of this book's proceeds are donated to the Hugo Bustamante AYSO Playership Fund, a national scholarship program to help ensure that no child misses the chance to play AYSO Soccer. Donations to the fund cover the cost of registration and a uniform for a child in need.

Text by Illugi Jökulsson
Design and layout: Árni Torfason

For the English-language edition
Copy editor: Ashley Benning
Production editor: Matt Garczynski
Composition: Ada Rodriguez
Production manager: Louise Kurtz

PHOTOGRAPHY CREDITS

Getty Images: front cover left (Dennis Grombkowski/Bongarts), front cover middle (Matthew Stockman), front cover right (Michael Regan), p. 10 (George Tiedemann/Sports Illustrated), pp. 12–13 and back cover middle (Tommy Cheng/AFP), p. 14 (George Tiedemann/Sports Illustrated), pp. 16–17 (George Tiedemann), pp. 18–19 (Jed Jacobsohn), pp. 20–21 (A. Messerschmidt), pp. 22–23 (Simon Bruty/Sports Illustrated), p. 25 and back cover top (Boris Streubel), pp. 26–27 (Adam Pretty/FIFA), pp. 28–29 (Stuart Franklin/FIFA), pp. 30–31 (William Volcov/Brazil Photo Press/Latin-Content), p. 32 (VI Images), p. 33 middle (Dennis Grombkowski/Bongarts), p. 33 bottom (Patrick McDermott/Stringer), p. 34 (Ronny Hartmann/Bongarts), p. 35 top (Maja Hitj), p. 35 bottom (Hannah Peters), p. 36 middle (Mike Hewitt/FIFA), p. 36 bottom (Athena Pictures), p. 37 (Ben Radford), p. 38 left (Eric Verhoevan/Soccrates), p. 38 right (TF-Images), p. 39 left (Martin Rose), p. 39 right (Christopher Lee), p. 40 left (Popperfoto), p. 40 right (Tony Feder), p. 41 (Rich Lam), p. 43 top (Steve Christo/Corbis), p. 43 bottom (Naomi Baker), p. 48 (Gualter Fatia), p. 50 (Mike Zarrilli), p. 51 (Omar Vega), p. 53 top (Ronald Martinez), p. 53 bottom (Mike Hewitt/FIFA), p. 54 (Robbie Jay Barratt), p. 56 (Meg Oliphant), p. 57 and back cover bottom (Jared Wickerham), p. 58 (Tom Dulat), p. 59 top (Scott Halleran)

Wikimedia Commons: pp. 6–7, p. 8 left, p. 8 right (Антон Зайцев), p.9 (Валерий Дед), p. 36 top (Katie Chan), p. 52 (Soccerfan1996), p. 59 bottom (Jamie Smed)

Shutterstock: p. 33 top (Oleksandr Osipov), p. 42 (Oleksandr Osipov), pp. 44–45 (Lev Radin), pp. 46–47 (Lev Radin), p. 49 (Lev Radin), pp. 60–61 (Lev Radin), p. 55 (Lev Radin)

First published in the United States of America in 2019 by Abbeville Press, 655 Third Avenue, New York, NY 10017

First Edition
10 9 8 7 6 5 4 3 2 1

ISBN 978-0-7892-1328-0

Library of Congress Cataloging-in-Publication Data available upon request

For bulk and premium sales and for text adoption procedures, write to Customer Service Manager, Abbeville Press, 655 Third Avenue, New York, NY 10017, or call 1-800-ARTBOOK.

Visit Abbeville Press online at www.abbeville.com.

CONTENTS

THE HOST COU

The 2019 edition of the FIFA Women's World Cup will be held in a country whose culture, fashion, cooking, literature, and music continue to influence people the world over.

In ancient times France was called Gaul, a part of Celtic Europe until the region was conquered by Julius Caesar in the name of the Roman Empire. In the Middle Ages, France became an independent kingdom and with time grew into one of great powers of Europe. France played a considerable role in helping a budding United States break free from British rule, and in turn, American ideas of emancipation inspired the French to revolt against the Bourdon regime in 1789. Emperor Napoleon made France the reigning power in Europe at the beginning of the 19th century but was eventually toppled by the nation's enemies. France nevertheless remained a powerful country and snatched its share of colonies around the globe, not least in Africa—the birthplace of many of France's most talented soccer stars. During the 20th century, France's stability was greatly threatened by the two world wars and the country needed aid from the United States to defend itself against Germany. Modern France is a leader in the European Union.

Joan of Arc at the Coronation of Charles VII, by Jean Auguste Dominique Ingres in 1854

Gauguin, c. 1891

Joan of Arc (1412–1431)
This teenage girl emboldened the French people in their struggle against the English during the Hundred Years' War.

Louis XIV (1638–1715)
The Sun King lived a lavish lifestyle in the Palace of Versailles longer than any other European monarch.

Voltaire (1694–1778)
One of the major thinkers of the Enlightenment in the 18th century, he contributed to a new way of thinking that divorced itself from outdated and dogmatic religious ideas.

Napoleon (1769–1821)
Known for epic feats on the battlefield and political reforms, not least in relation to law, his fall from grace was steep.

Napoleon's Return from Elba, by Charles de Steuben

Coco Chanel (1883–1971) Famous fashion designer whose influence spread over the early 20th century. She emphasized fashion that was both practical and durable.

Louis Pasteur (1822–1895)
An incredibly important figure in the field of medicine, Pasteur developed vaccinations and treatments for dangerous diseases.

Paul Gauguin (1848–1903)
This Post-Impressionist was one of many fantastic French painters. Paris was the hub of culture and arts for many decades.

Simone de Beauvoir (1908–1986)
France has given birth to many thinkers and philosophers. Beauvoir's writings inspired a new movement fighting for women's rights.

Edith Piaf (1915–1963)
Édith "the Little Sparrow" Piaf made music that drew on French folk and pop songs framed in her highly personal and emotional style.

Brigitte Bardot (born 1934)
This film star who was perhaps not the world's greatest actress but still inspired ideas of the new and free woman of the late 20th century.

Yves Saint Laurent (1936–2008)
He carried on the legacy of French fashion innovators Chanel and Christian Dior and elevated it to an even higher level, at the same time making prêt-à-porter (ready-to-wear clothes) respectable.

FRANCE IS 248,572 SQUARE MILES, MAKING IT THE 42ND LARGEST COUNTRY IN THE WORLD. COMPARABLE IN SIZE TO AFGHANISTAN OR SOMALIA, IT IS THE NEXT LARGEST COUNTRY AFTER RUSSIA, IF OVERSEAS TERRITORIES ARE ALSO COUNTED. IT IS AROUND 35% THE SIZE OF ALASKA, SLIGHTLY SMALLER THAN TEXAS, YET CONSIDERABLY LARGER THAN CALIFORNIA.

POPULATION 67 MILLION

FRANCE IS THE 20TH MOST POPULOUS COUNTRY IN THE WORLD, SIMILAR TO THAILAND AND GREAT BRITAIN. IT IS THIRD MOST POPULOUS COUNTRY IN EUROPE FOLLOWING RUSSIA AND GERMANY. FRANCE HAS ALMOST TWICE AS MANY RESIDENTS AS THE MOST POPULOUS US STATE, CALIFORNIA, AT 40 MILLION.

LARGEST CITIES		POPULATION
1	PARIS	2.2 MILLION, SIMILAR TO HOUSTON, TEXAS
2	MARSEILLES	855,000, SIMILAR TO CHARLOTTE, NORTH CAROLINA
3	LYON	500,000, SIMILAR TO SACRAMENTO, CALIFORNIA
4	TOULOUSE	458,000, SIMILAR TO MIAMI, FLORIDA
5	NICE	342,000, SIMILAR TO HONOLULU, HAWAII

MEN'S WORLD CUP

The French national team has achieved many successes at the men's World Cup tournament over the years.

1998

Zinedine Zidane, a graceful and sophisticated midfielder, led France to its first World Cup title on home turf. In the final, Zidane scored two goals with headers in a 3–0 demolition of Brazil.

1958

Just Fontaine

Just Fontaine scored 13 goals in the 1958 World Cup in Sweden. It is a World Cup record that remains unsurpassed.

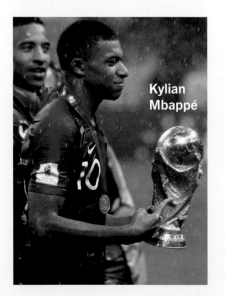

Kylian Mbappé

2018

Kylian Mbappé, despite being only 19, was the most dynamic attacking force in France's second World Cup victory in Russia. France beat Croatia 4–2 in the final.

THE VENUES

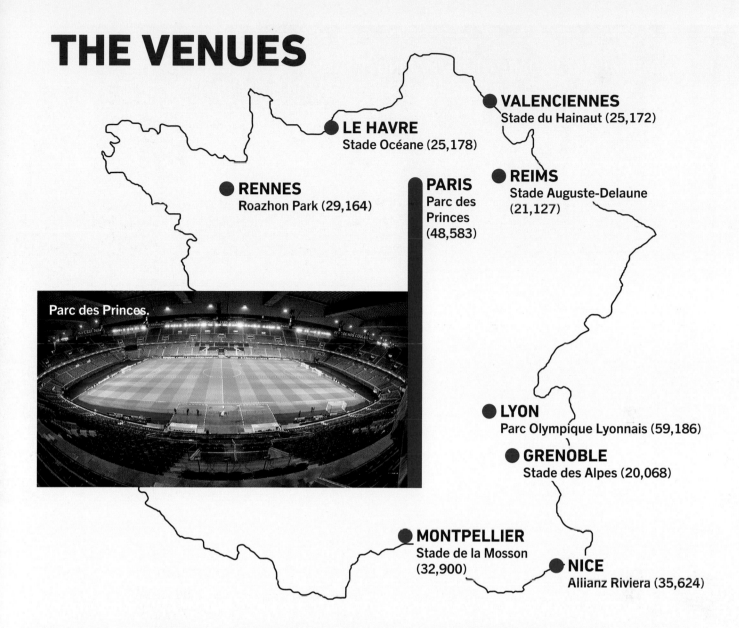

VALENCIENNES
Stade du Hainaut (25,172)

LE HAVRE
Stade Océane (25,178)

RENNES
Roazhon Park (29,164)

PARIS
Parc des Princes (48,583)

REIMS
Stade Auguste-Delaune (21,127)

Parc des Princes.

LYON
Parc Olympique Lyonnais (59,186)

GRENOBLE
Stade des Alpes (20,068)

MONTPELLIER
Stade de la Mosson (32,900)

NICE
Allianz Riviera (35,624)

THE FIFA WOMEN'S WORLD CUP

A total of 24 countries will compete at the 2019 World Cup in France. Along with the hosts, the competition will see eight European nations, one from Oceania, five from Asia, three from South America, three from North America, Central America and the Caribbean (CONCACAF), as well as three from Africa.

The teams will be divided into six groups of four for the group stage. Two winners of each group then move on to the knockout round. These 12 teams are joined there by the four other teams that gave the best performance in third place of each group stage. The 16 teams will compete until the last one standing can be named, the new world champion!

The group stage will begin on June 7, 2019, with the first game of the knockout stage to follow on June 22. The final will be held in Lyon on July 7.

Will the three-time Cup winner and defending US team make it to the top again? Will three-time champion Germany or 2011 winner Japan reassert themselves? Or will a new powerhouse take the prize in 2019?

Michelle
Akers

WOMEN'S WORLD CUP

WORLD CUP 1991

Women's soccer was a common pastime at the beginning of the twentieth century, particularly in England. Sometimes thousands of spectators would attend games between women's teams. The sport was also gaining popularity across the Atlantic in the United States. However, around 1920, the English Football Association took measures to sideline women's soccer. These men came together and simply decided that the sport was not feminine, and the following 50 years saw hardly any organized women's soccer.

Around 1970, things began to take a different turn. In 1985, US women's national team played its first international match, losing 0–1 to Italy. This was unquestionably progress, and the first FIFA Women's World Cup was held in China six years later in November 1991 with the US team clearly a fan favorite.

The US had come out on top of the 1991 CONCACAF Women's Championship tournament for North and Central America and the Caribbean as their ticket to the 1991 World Cup. Nineteen-year-old Mia Hamm scored the first goal for the women's national team, but then the older and more experienced women took over. Michelle Akers scored 11 goals in five games, April Heinrichs scored 10, and Brandi Chastain seven.

When the World Cup kicked off in China on November 16, the US faced stiff competition in its very first game of the group stage, but then proceeded to defeat Sweden 3–2, with two goals coming from the fierce Carin Jennings and one scored by Mia Hamm. The US breezed through the next two games: 5–0 against Brazil (Heinrichs two goals; Akers, Jennings and Hamm with one each) and 3–0 against Japan with Akers making two goals and Wendy Gebauer one.

The winning streak continued with a smooth 7–0 win against Chinese Taipei (Taiwan) in the quarterfinals. Akers scored a whopping five goals, while Julie Foudy and Joy Fawcett got one each. Although a tough battle was predicted for US v. Germany in the semifinals, Jennings blasted the team to a 3–0 lead in the first three minutes, with Heinrichs adding another two in the second half. The game ended with a tremendous 5–2 win for the US, securing a place in the final.

THE FIRST US TITLE

The three-time world champion Pelé attended the first Women's World Cup final as an honorary guest to watch the US face off against Norway. The Scandinavian countries were among the first pioneers of women's soccer, and Norway had defeated first Denmark and then Sweden for Nordic dominance during the run-up to the final. In the 20th minute, Akers rose above the Norwegian defense to head home a soaring free kick from Shannon Higgins. Norway refused to give up, and Linda Medalen scored a strikingly similar goal only nine minutes later. This was the beginning of a brutal struggle. Both teams had great opportunities to score; however, it was only at the 78th minute that Akers received a dashing long pass, again from Higgins, outsmarted two Norwegian defenders, and with a final trick pulled on the goalkeeper was able to power the ball into the exposed goal. With a mesmerizing and worthy final goal, the United States became the first champion of the Women's World Cup.

1991 FIFA WOMEN'S WORLD CUP FINAL

DATE: NOVEMBER 30, 1991
VENUE: TIANHE STADIUM, GUANGZHOU, CHINA
ATTENDANCE: 63,000

USA – NORWAY
2–1

AKERS 20	MEDALEN 29
AKERS 78	

MARY HARVEY
MIA HAMM – CARLA OVERBECK – JOY FAWCETT
LINDA HAMILTON
SHANNON HIGGINS – JULIE FOUDY – KRISTINE LILLY
APRIL HEINRICHS – MICHELLE AKERS – CARIN JENNINGS

COACH: ANSON DORRANCE

Mia
Hamm

WORLD CUP 1995

The US victory at the 1991 World Cup failed to attract the attention it deserved at home. Women's soccer was still off the radar for a majority of sports fans. The team, unfazed by this lack of interest, continued to develop and grow stronger. Coach Tony DiCicco brought a remarkably robust team to the 1995 World Cup in Sweden, but the women would be in for a shock. The seemingly infallible Michelle Akers suffered an injury in the first game against China and mostly had to sit out the following games. Tisha Venturini, Tiffeny Milbrett, and Mia Hamm gave the US a 3–1 lead but the tenacious Chinese managed to even out the score at the end of the first half. Later, the US won comfortably against Denmark (2–0 with goals by Milbrett and Kristine Lilly) and then Australia (4–1 with goals by Julie Foudy, Joy Fawcett, Carla Overbeck and Debbie Keller).

Everything went without a hitch during the quarterfinals with the US demolishing Japanese team 4–0.

The incredible Lilly delivered an outstanding performance, scoring two goals with Milbrett and Venturini scoring the rest. In the semifinals, however, things quickly went south against Norway. The Norwegians scored early on and managed to ward off numerous US offensive attempts, and the US hopes for a second title came to an abrupt end. Venturini and Hamm went on to score the two goals of a 2–0 victory over China to land the WNT in third place. Norway faced off against Germany for the final, with Germany winning 2–0.

The US avenged the Norwegian debacle a year later when women competed in soccer for the first time at the 1996 Summer Olympics, held in Atlanta. The US bested Norway 2–1 in the semifinals with goals scored by Akers and Shannon MacMillan. Milbrett and MacMillan then both scored in a 2–1 win against China in the final in Athens, Georgia.

WORLD CUP 1999

The 1999 World Cup was a turning point for women's soccer worldwide. The organizers of the tournament managed to stir up a level of enthusiasm and attention that was enough to put women's soccer on the map for the first time. Now everybody was talking about it, including fans in the United States.

Tony DiCicco served again as the WNT coach again and drew on the strengths of the solid team that had been forming over the previous years. The first US goal in the tournament was scored by no other than the spirited Mia Hamm. She easily swiveled around the defense and launched a powerful shot that flew right past the goalkeeper. Julie Foudy and Kristine Lilly also scored for a 3–0 win against the tough Danish team.

What followed was the biggest World Cup achievement for the WNT yet: a 7–1 pulverization of the Nigerian team. The first point for the US came from an own goal by Nigeria, but the team took over the initiative by racking up proper ones, scored by Hamm, Tiffeny Milbrett (two), Lilly, Michelle Akers, and Cindy Parlow. The American team played like a well-oiled machine in this game, and likewise in the tournament as a whole. It should be mentioned that Nigeria also performed well overall, making it to the quarterfinals where it just barely lost to Brazil.

After beating North Korea 3–0, with two goals scored by Tisha Venturini and one by Shannon MacMillan, the US met with a sturdy and resilient German team.

Milbrett scored in the first half, but Germany had gained a 2–1 lead when the whistle was blown for halftime. Defender Brandi Chastain was unfortunate enough to give Germany one of its points with an own goal. During the second half, Chastain made amends by leveling the score. Joy Fawcett then proceeded to head in the winning goal to land the US in the semifinals. President Bill Clinton himself attended the game, a clear sign of how far the Women's World Cup had climbed on the ladder of respect.

In the semifinals, the US easily beat an energetic and belligerent Brazil. Parlow scored the first goal with a header and Akers the next one on a penalty kick. Brazil had numerous chances to try to come back, but a stalwart Briana Scurry confidently kept all their efforts away from the American goal.

Mia
Hamm

17

THE SECOND US TITLE

The Chinese team the US faced in the 1999 World Cup final was no pushover. China had won all their games with ease, for instance by overwhelming the defending champions Norway 5–0 in the semifinals. China's superb striker Sun Wen already had seven goals in the bag, and the American players knew that if they could find a way to stop Wen, they would be that much closer to victory. The game attracted major global attention, with record attendance for a women-only sporting event and 40 million TV viewers the world over. The match was a rugged and laborious battle with both teams emphasizing a solid defense rather than offense. No goals were scored in normal time, but overtime saw a thundering header from Fan Yunjie, which Lilly defended with a glorious header of her own. Now the game would have to be settled with a shoot-out. Scurry saved China's third spot kick, so when Brandi Chastain stepped forward, the score hovering at 4–4, she was the team's last chance. She coolly made the shot, and in one stroke the US clinched the world championship title, for the second time.

1999 FIFA WOMEN'S WORLD CUP FINAL
DATE: JULY 10, 1999
VENUE: ROSE BOWL, PASADENA, CALIFORNIA
ATTENDANCE: 90,000

USA—CHINA
0–0 (AET)

5–4 (PENALTIES)
OVERBECK 1–1 XIE HUILIN
FAWCETT 1–1 QUI HAIYAN
LILLY 1–0 LIU YING
HAMM 1–1 ZHANG OUYING
CHASTAIN 1–1 SUN WEN

BRIANA SCURRY
JOY FAWCETT – CARLA OVERBECK – KATE SOBRERO – BRANDI CHASTAIN
JULIE FOUDY – MICHELLE AKERS (SARA WHALEN 91) – KRISTINE LILLY
MIA HAMM – CINDY PARLOW (SHANNON MACMILLAN 57) – TIFFENY MILBRETT
(TISHA VENTURINI 115)

COACH: TONY DICICCO

WORLD CUP 2003

The US world champions were forced to accept a bitter loss at the final of the 2000 Summer Olympics in Sydney. Tiffeny Milbrett scored two goals, but it fell short of a lead and Norway won 3–2. In 2003, this only made the US even more determined to defend the World Cup title in a tournament on home soil. Serving as coach was the 1991 legend April Heinrichs, and the US arrived with a team largely made up of veterans of the 1999 World Cup. The most notable newcomer was an exceptionally dynamic and powerful forward from New York, Abby Wambach. Midfielder Shannon Boxx would also later become an important pillar of the WNT.

The group stage went like a dream. Kristine Lilly, Cindy Parlow, and Boxx scored the goals in a near-effortless 3–1 win against Sweden. Mia Hamm scored two goals, Parlow and Wambach one each, and then captain Julie Foudy in a 5–0 shutout of the Nigerian team. The last game was against North Korea, and Wambach scored first with a penalty kick, followed by two goals from newcomer and defender Cat Whitehill. The US won 3–0.

In the quarterfinals, Wambach's only goal was enough to overcome Norway. The US then faced European champion Germany in the semifinals with legend Birgit Prinz at the height of her form. Germany scored an early goal with a header, and no matter how relentlessly the American players tried to equalize, the ball refused to find the net. During overtime, Germany scored twice on the counterattack and thus the world champions were knocked out with a 0–3 defeat. An easy win against Canada in the battle for third place was a mild consolation. Lilly, Boxx, and Milbrett took care of the scoring.

In the end, Germany snatched the World Cup title through a 2–1 win in the overtime final against Sweden.

Mia Hamm and
Abby Wambach

WORLD CUP 2007

The US performed well at the 2004 Summer Olympics in Athens. The "old guard" of Mia Hamm, Julie Foudy, Joy Fawcett, and Brandi Chastain was still going strong, with Christie Rampone building a strong defense and Abby Wambach freely racking up goals. It seemed only fitting that Wambach scored the winning goal in the final against Brazil. Prior to this, the US had effortlessly beaten both Japan and Germany in the knockout stage.

As usual the US sent a mighty team to the 2007 World Cup tournament, held in China. A new coach was at the helm, Greg Ryan. Although the old guard had now mostly retired, veteran powerhouse Kristine Lilly remained as team captain. Expectations for the team were soaring. What garnered most attention was that the fiery Hope Solo replaced Briana Scurry in the goal for part of the tournament. Another newcomer entered the stage, who would go on to make a big splash in soccer world also made an appearance, the 25-year-old Carli Lloyd.

In the group stage, the US and North Korea tied, 2–2, with goals from Abby Wambach and Heather O'Reilly. The US then defeated Sweden 2–0, Wambach scoring twice, and then barely beat Nigeria 1–0 with the game's only goal coming from Lori Chalupny in the first minute.

In the quarterfinals, the US swept England with a 3–0 win, with goals being scored by Wambach, Shannon Boxx, and Lilly. In the semifinals, the US team went head-to-head with Brazil. Coach Ryan made a controversial decision to replace Solo in the goal with veteran Scurry, arguing that she was better suited to handle the technicality of the Brazilians. Although the US had battled through 50 games undefeated, but Brazil played brilliantly and won 4–0, with the US losing Boxx to a red card just before halftime.

A 4–1 win against Norway gave the US third place, with Wambach scoring twice and Chalupny and O'Reilly scoring the rest. Brazil would go on to be blanked by Germany 2–0 in the final.

Kristine
Lilly

23

WORLD CUP 2011

The US team arrived in Germany with a new coach, the Swedish Pia Sundhage, and a host of powerful players making their World Cup debut. Some had participated in the effort to defend the Olympic gold at Beijing 2008 in which Carli Lloyd scored the only goal of the final against Brazil. Many of the new teammates would turn out to play an imperative role in Germany and for years to come. Among them were Becky Sauerbrunn, Rachel Buehler, and Ali Krieger in defensive positions; Kelley O'Hara, Megan Rapinoe and Tobin Heath midfield; and forwards Lauren Cheney and the young Alex Morgan.

The US first squared off against North Korea, making it the fourth time these teams faced each other in the group round of the World Cup. Buehler and Cheney both landed a goal, and the game ended with a 2–0 victory for the US.

The next game against Colombia was child's play. Heather O'Reilly, Rapinoe, and Carli Lloyd scored three goals and easily sealed the victory.

With this positive momentum, the third game was a great shock as the US team was mowed down by their coach's own compatriots, the ever-powerful Swedes. The US played unevenly during the first half and conceded two goals to Sweden. Although Abby Wambach managed to stir up some hope with one goal just before halftime, it was ultimately not enough.

The US came in second in their group after Sweden. In the quarterfinals the Americans then landed a tough opponent, in Brazil, with Marta Vieira da Silva in tremendous form. The Brazilians scored an own goal early in the game and the US was in the lead but Marta scored an equalizer with a penalty kick. A red card sent Buehler off soon after. A player short against an energetic and fiery Brazil is no cakewalk, but the US put up a good fight and played with great determination. During overtime, Marta gave Brazil the lead but Wambach replied with a goal, and time was called with the score at 2–2. The American women showed no mercy in the penalty shoot-out and Shannon Boxx, Lloyd, Wambach, Rapinoe, and Krieger all scored. Hope Solo defended a shot and thereby ensured the US a place in the semifinals.

Now the US was faced with the rapidly improving French team. In the ninth minute, Cheney tapped the ball in after a cross from O'Reilly. France leveled the game at the start of the second half, but Wambach later scored a header intercepting a corner kick from Cheney. Morgan then flipped the ball into the goal after a strong offense, and the US made it back to the final for the first time in 12 years.

Carli
Lloyd

THE FINAL

The US squared off with Japan in the final. The Japanese team had already surprised the world with a highly impressive and powerful performance in the tournament. Japan had sent the German and Swedish powerhouses packing. Still, many now believed that the incredible energy of the Japanese had dried up. Abby Wambach botched a chance to score and so did Alex Morgan, but a US goal seemed imminent. Morgan finally managed to put the ball into the net following a rush offense. A defensive mishap by the US allowed Japan to secure an equalizer just moments before regular time ran out, expanding play to the inevitable overtime. Wambach began by scoring a trademark goal with a thundering header off a pass from Morgan and the US seemed ready to embrace the title. However, a few minutes before the final whistle, the Japanese once again squeezed in an equalizer on a corner kick. Victory would now have to come from a shoot-out. Luck was not with the US team here: O'Reilly, Lloyd, and Heath failed, and though Wambach managed a goal, it was already over. Japan dominated the shootout 3–1 and was thereby crowned the new world champion, leaving the world stunned.

WORLD CUP 2015

The US was able to avenge itself against Japan with a 2–1 victory in the 2012 Olympic Games final, held in London. It was the national team's fourth gold. Carli Lloyd scored both goals in what seemed a smooth win.

Despite a high place on FIFA Women's Ranking List, the US team had failed to clinch a World Cup title in 16 years. The US competed for a slot in the 2015 FIFA Women's World Cup in the 2014 CONCACAF Women's Championship, which awarded three places to the tournament in Canada the following year. Trinidad and Tobago's team put up a tough fight in the first game, but a goal from Abby Wambach during the second half finally sealed a US victory. The win set a straight course for the US, and the team went on to easily defeat Guatemala 5–0 and Haiti 6–0. The US easily beat Mexico 3–0 in the semifinals and then crushed Costa Rica 6–0 in the final. Wambach scored four goals in the game and was the tournament's top goal scorer at seven goals. Carli Lloyd scored five.

In the beginning of July, a new coach, Jill Ellis, traveled with the team to Canada for the 2015 World Cup. By now the team boasted significant depth. Christie Rampone was 39 years old and had played 306 national games. If the US team could make it far enough into the tournament, it was clear that Rampone would be able to celebrate her 40th birthday while still playing for the WNT. Her pace was beginning to slow, but she was still captain of the team and an integral part of it.

In the first game, the US beat Australia with ease 3–1. Megan Rapinoe shone and scored two goals with Christen Press scoring the third. Press, Meghan Klingenberg, and Julie Ertz were the big names of the tournament in Canada, even though they had all played in less than 50 international games.

Next matchup was against Sweden, this time led by former US coach Pia Sundhage. The battle was fierce, with a final score of 0–0.

The last game of the group round was against Nigeria. A corner pass from Rapinoe allowed Wambach to fire a beautiful goal into the net just moments before halftime. That was it, despite Nigeria losing a player in the second half. The WNT had conquered their group.

Christen
Press

THE KNOCKOUT STAGE

In 2015, the Women's World Cup expanded to include more teams, and a round of 16 was added to the schedule for the knockout round. The US team confronted Colombia in the round of 16 and a great struggle ensued. The Colombian goalkeeper knocked down Alex Morgan just outside the penalty area and was sent off as a result. Abby Wambach's penalty shot barely missed the goal. Morgan broke the stalemate in the 53rd minute, and Carli Lloyd scored another with a penalty kick in the 66th minute after Megan Rapinoe had taken a hit. In the quarterfinals, both Lauren Cheney Holiday and Rapinoe were suspended during a game against China. The US was relentless on offense, but the only goal arrived in the 51st minute. Julie Johnston catapulted a long pass and Lloyd headed the ball into the net.

The team had advanced to the semifinals, and the opponent was of the fiercest kind, the European champion Germany with its most powerful team yet. Both teams played as safely as possible. Germany got a penalty kick early on in the first half, but the legendary Célia Šašić failed to deliver. The pressure was now on Lloyd when a German defender got a penalty for taking down Morgan in the 69th minute, and she did not disappoint. Germany went for an equalizer but in the 84th minute substitute Kelly O'Hara scored the US's second goal following a pass from Lloyd.

The US advanced to the finals for its second World Cup tournament in a row. The team would face none other than the defending champion Japan, which had beaten the Netherlands, Australia, and England during the knockout phase.

Notice anything special about Carli Lloyd's uniform? While playing as team captain, Lloyd wears the traditional blue captain's armband to signify her role. Any player can be captain, no matter their position, and for the US's final three matches of the 2015 World Cup the role fell to Carli Lloyd. During the final, however, the team subbed in their beloved star forward Abby Wambach, who was coming to the end of her 15-year international career. In a heartwarming gesture of respect, Lloyd ran over and handed the armband to Wambach as she came onto the World Cup stage for the final time. And after the team secured its victory, Wambach in turn passed the armband to team elder Christie Rampone.

Carli
Lloyd

THE THIRD US TITLE

Those expecting a thrilling and hard-fought World Cup final in 2015 were in for a serious disappointment. Carli Lloyd had become increasingly prominent over the course of the tournament and was now captain as Abby Wambach took on a more defensive role. Lloyd was brimming with self-confidence. Only three minutes into the game, Megan Rapinoe made a swift corner pass and Lloyd blasted the ball into the net. This was the fastest goal in a Women's World Cup final, and only two minutes later Lloyd struck again, assisted by Lauren Cheney Holiday, to slide the ball past Japan's goalkeeper. The Japanese were shell-shocked, which allowed Holiday to outwit the stunned defenders and score the third goal in the 14th minute. A couple minutes later, Lloyd pulled off a hat trick with one of the most remarkable goals in World Cup history, counting both men and women. She received the ball near the halfway line, her eyes fixed on the Japanese goalkeeper at the other end of the field. Lloyd went for it, with a precision blast and the ball sped through the air, over the goalkeeper, and right into the net. This was the first hat trick in the history of World Cup finals since Geoff Hearst's for England in 1966. After 16 minutes the score stood at 4–0! To the team's credit, Japan refused to surrender and managed two goals before Tobin Heath sealed the deal for the US with another successful effort in the 54th minute. As the Japanese team finally began to wilt, the American fans were already celebrating in the stands.

It was an outstanding and historic victory, thoroughly deserved.

2015 FIFA WOMEN'S WORLD CUP FINAL
DATE: JULY 5, 2015
VENUE: BC PLACE, VANCOUVER, CANADA
ATTENDANCE: 53,000

USA—JAPAN
5–2

CARLI LLOYD 3	YUKI OGIMI 27
CARLI LLOYD 5	JULIE JOHNSTON (OWN GOAL) 52
LAUREN CHENEY HOLIDAY 14	
CARLI LLOYD 16	
TOBIN HEATH 54	

HOPE SOLO
ALI KRIEGER – JULIE JOHNSTON ERTZ – BECKY SAUERBRUNN
MEGHAN KLINGENBERG
TOBIN HEATH (ABBY WAMBACH 79) – LAUREN CHENEY HOLIDAY
MORGAN BRIAN – MEGAN RAPINOE (KELLEY O'HARA 61)
ALEX MORGAN (CHRISTIE RAMPONE 86) – CARLI LLOYD

COACH: JILL ELLIS

US'S TOP RIVALS IN 2019

FRANCE

For nearly a decade, the French national team has attracted attention for both skilled and cunning players and an intelligent, entertaining, and elegant style. The only problem is the team has never gone the distance. Aside from fourth place at the 2011 World Cup and in the 2012 Summer Olympics, France has never made it beyond the quarterfinals in any major tournament. The generation that has recently carried the torch for France is still in their prime. It's do-or-die time for the women's national team to claim the World Cup title, just as the men did in Moscow in 2018.

Wendie Renard is an unusually graceful player and not only because of her towering height (she is 6 ft 1.5 in). She was born on the small Caribbean island of Martinique and has served as a stalwart defender for Lyon in the French league. Sarah Bouhaddi, Lyon and the WNT goalkeeper, is also a force to be reckoned with.

Amandine Henry left Lyon in 2016 and played with Portland Thorns for a time, among other teams. Henry is a driven and dynamic midfielder who has now returned to Lyon and assumed the position of captain of the national team. She is determined to play her part in guaranteeing a world championship for the women's team.

France has some outstanding goal scorers in their ranks, such as Marie-Laure Delie and Gaëtane Thiney, but the standout is Lyon's Eugénie Le Sommer. She is short but lightning quick and agile like a cat, with incredible shooting power. She will be a top contender for the 2019 Golden Boot.

WENDIE RENARD
BORN 1990
DEFENDER
NATIONAL GAMES 101
GOALS 19

SARAH BOUHADDI
BORN 1986
GOALKEEPER
NATIONAL GAMES 131

AMANDINE HENRY
BORN 1989
PLAYMAKER
NATIONAL GAMES 76
GOALS 11

EUGÉNIE LE SOMMER
BORN 1989
STRIKER
NATIONAL GAMES 154
GOALS 74

GERMANY

Ever since 1989, the German team has been nearly unstoppable at European Championship tournaments. The team also clinched the World Cup title in both 2003 and 2007 and Olympic gold in Rio de Janeiro in 2016. Germany has amassed 11 tournament titles, along with one silver medal and three bronze. The team is without a doubt a fan favorite and with high aspirations for the World Cup in France, but a creeping worry looms over coach Martina Voss. Although the team lost only two games in 2018, both these defeats were at the hands of their main competitors at the 2019 World Cup: France and the United States.

Germany has undergone some turnover in recent years, but the backbone of the team is still veteran players such as defensive bulwark Babett Peter, midfielders Lena Goessling and Leonie Maier, and the relentless forward Alexandra Popp. The national team benefits from the fact that the German league is one of Europe's strongest, and powerhouse teams such as Wolfsburg and Bayern München provide a venue for some of the toughest women soccer players in the country. They can anticipate each other's moves so that the team plays like a well-oiled machine. Many attacking midfielders will fight hard for their place on the German national team to help lay claim to Germany's first World Cup title in 12 years.

The Hungarian-born Dzsenifer Marozsán is perhaps Germany's pivotal player. She dominates the midfield and has a keen eye for passes and game strategy. Many consider her to be the world's greatest playmaker. But she also possesses enough power and determination to break through the defense and rack up the goals.

ALEXANDRA POPP
BORN 1991
STRIKER
NATIONAL GAMES 91
GOALS 44

BABETT PETER
BORN 1988
DEFENDER
NATIONAL GAMES 118
GOALS 8

DZSENIFER MAROZSÁN
BORN 1992
PLAYMAKER
NATIONAL GAMES 86
GOALS 32

35

ENGLAND

Though women's soccer was very popular in England from 1880 to 1920, the sport took a while to regain prestige after 50 years of neglect. But in recent years, the English women's national team has risen to become one of Europe's top contenders and third on the FIFA Women's Ranking List. England won the bronze medal at the 2015 World Cup in Canada, after beating Norway, Canada and Germany. The team's recent success is largely due to the part played by two powerful defenders: Steph Houghton and Lucy Bronze. The latter now counts among the world's greatest players and is part of the multiple award-winning French team Lyon, where her attacking spirit, precision passes, and long shots get free rein. The English forward Jodie Taylor has had a comeback recently, playing with numerous teams around the globe, for instance in Canada and the US.

STEPH HOUGHTON
BORN 1988
DEFENDER
INTERNATIONAL GAMES 86
GOALS 11

LUCY BRONZE
BORN 1991
RIGHT BACK
INTERNATIONAL GAMES 60
GOALS 7

JODIE TAYLOR
BORN 1986
STRIKER
INTERNATIONAL GAMES 38
GOALS 17

CHRISTINE SINCLAIR
BORN 1983
PLAYMAKER, FORWARD
INTERNATIONAL GAMES 274
GOALS 177

CANADA

Although Canada has often stood in the shadow of its mighty neighbor to the south, the team has recently shown growing promise on the international stage. The Canadians are fortunate enough to boast one of the world's top players, born in one of the suburbs of Vancouver, British Columbia. She has served as a major pillar of the national team ever since her first international game in 2000, at the tender age of 17. Said player is no other than Christine Sinclair, an athletic, sharp, and thundering forward and ingenious playmaker. Her versatility and skills have no limits.

Sinclair's passing accuracy is the stuff of legends and so is her reading of the game.

NETHERLANDS

Only a decade ago the Dutch team was considered mediocre at best. The team only managed to reach the European Championship in 2009 and the World Cup not until 2015. However, something magical must have happened there recently because the country is now producing one wizardly player after the other.

To everyone's surprise, the Dutch team was crowned the European champions on home soil in 2017, and the 2019 World Cup team will be equipped with two of the world's most powerful forwards.

Lieke Martens was no soccer wunderkind. She played for a series of second-rate teams in Europe before showing up on the world stage out of nowhere at the 2017 Euro. Her attacking spirit, ingenious passes, and focus made her one of the Netherlands' most lethal weapons. She was selected Player of the Tournament as well as receiving the Bronze Boot for scoring four goals, two of which were in the final against Denmark.

Vivianne Miedema is young and still progressing, but she she can score goals of every possible variety almost at will.

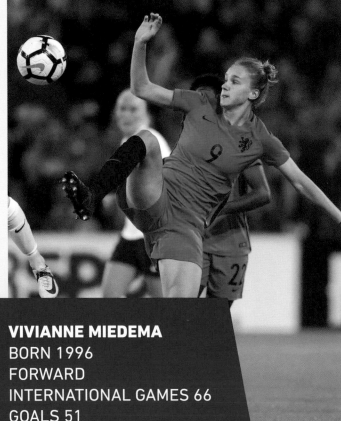

LIEKE MARTENS
BORN 1992
FORWARD
INTERNATIONAL GAMES 95
GOALS 39

VIVIANNE MIEDEMA
BORN 1996
FORWARD
INTERNATIONAL GAMES 66
GOALS 51

CAROLINE SEGER
BORN 1985
MIDFIELDER
INTERNATIONAL GAMES 163
GOALS 23

STINA BLACKSTENIUS
BORN 1996
STRIKER
INTERNATIONAL GAMES 26
GOALS 5

SWEDEN

The Swedes were pioneers of women's soccer in Europe. In 1984, Sweden won the first ever Euro Women competition. Only 16 teams participated in qualifiers that year and four teams played in the final tournament. Each game was 70 minutes, and the soccer ball used is nowadays intended for children aged 9–14. Sweden's victory came easily, with raging support from Swedish soccer fans. The Swedish league is probably Europe's strongest, along with Germany and France, and has a strong following at home. Despite the tenacity of the national team, however, 2019 will mark 35 years since Sweden has taken first place in a major tournament. Their fans believe that it is their time now. Sweden managed to knock out the US in the quarterfinals at the 2016 Summer Olympics in Rio de Janeiro and then lost to Germany in the final after an even battle. Sweden has a tight core of veteran players, such as attacking midfielders Caroline Seger and Kosovare Asllani, defenders Nilla Fischer and Linda Sembrant, and goalkeeper Hedvig Lindahl. In addition, the 2019 World Cup will premiere the young and dynamic forwards Stina Blackstenius and Frida Rolfö.

BRAZIL

Contrary to popular opinion, the Brazilian team is not just "Marta and company." The fantastic Marta is certainly the team's dynamo and there are no signs of her calming down despite the 15 years since that have passed since she first leapt to the spotlight as one of the greatest women's soccer players in history. In October 2018, she was selected the Best FIFA Women's Player for the 6th time, and no player, whether male or female, has achieved this recognition as often as she has. Marta will turn 33 at the 2019 World Cup in France and though her speed has turned down just a notch, her cunning and shooting power are as potent as ever. Brazilians have remained indestructible in the Pan American Games and Copa América Feminina but the team has failed to reach the upper echelons of the World Cup. Marta will be the deciding factor in Brazil's success at the 2019 World Cup but among other great players on the team are the forward Cristiane Rozeira who, at the time of writing, has scored 90 goals in 120 international game.

The Brazilian team was set for high achievements at the 2015 World Cup in Canada and got off on a good start in the group stage. The team then suffered an horrific and somewhat surprising defeat at the hands of Australia. The tournament in France will present the last chance for Marta's generation to take home the

MARTA
BORN 1986
FORWARD
INTERNATIONAL GAMES 133
GOALS 110

CRISTIANE
BORN 1985
FORWARD
INTERNATIONAL GAMES 130
GOALS 90

SAKI KUMAGAI
BORN 1990
DEFENDER/DEFENSIVE MIDFIELDER
INTERNATIONAL GAMES 99
GOALS 0

JAPAN

Despite Japan's discouraging loss to the US team in the 2015 World Cup final, the Japanese team is nowhere close to giving up and will do everything it takes to rise to the top of 2019 tournament in France. Captain Saki Kumagai directs a stronghold defense and plays as a defensive midfielder with the world's best soccer club, the French team Lyon. Before 2011, Kumagai had never landed a goal even though she had played in numerous international games. The greatest moment of her career then presented itself when she finally managed to score the much-desired goal, during the shoot-out against the US at the 2011 World Cup, thereby serving Japan the cup. Goals in penalty shoot-outs are however not counted in FIFA rankings of international goals. Kumagai's will of steel and fighting spirit will nevertheless launch Japan far in the coming World Cup tournament.

NORWAY

Norwegian Ada Hegerberg is without a doubt the greatest forward of women's soccer history. Born in 1995, she is still young but has attracted worldwide attention for her sensational skills. She plays with the all-powerful French team Lyon and at the time of writing, Hegerberg has played 141 games for Lyon in four years and scored a whopping 177 goals. That was not a typo, the number is 177!

However, her situation also shows that despite the growing popularity and respect for women's soccer, the sport still has a long way to go. Norway has always belonged to the top tier from the very beginning. The Norwegian team won the Euro in both 1987 and 1993, went to the World Cup final in 1995, and clinched Olympic gold in 2000. But just as Norwegians have set their eyes on the highest prize, Hegerberg has come forward to express her disapproval about current developments in the sport. In an interview with the *Guardian* in Britain, she claimed that soccer "is the biggest sport in Norway for girls and has been for years but at the same time girls don't have the same opportunities as the boys." She also noted that despite Norway's history in women's soccer, things were getting tougher for girls. She had decided to retire from the national team and said she would not participate in the 2019 World Cup. It is clear that Norway will go to great lengths to convince their most prominent star to change her mind. Her absence will speak volumes on how far things still have to progress so that women players can feel equal to men. And it will be a great loss for Norway if she sticks by her decision.

ADA HEGERBERG
BORN 1995
STRIKER
NATIONAL GAMES 66
GOALS 38

AUSTRALIA

Australia has rapidly climbed the FIFA Women's Ranking List over recent years. And the agile and fierce forward Sam Kerr has played a major role in that rise. She has shown her talents for the Western New York Flash, Sky Blue FC, and Chicago Red Stars in the United States. Kerr's confidence and determined goal scoring attitude are often likened to Cristiano Ronaldo's, though Kerr herself rejects the comparison. Kerr celebrates her goals with a trademark backflip, and undoubtedly she will find an opportunity for another flip at the 2019 World Cup. In an interview with ABC. net she had this to say about the spirit of the Australian team, dubbed the Matildas: "The way that we play everyone can see that we are having fun . . . we work hard first and foremost, but we also enjoy it. We love being a part of this team and we love representing Australia, and we think we represent Australia well."

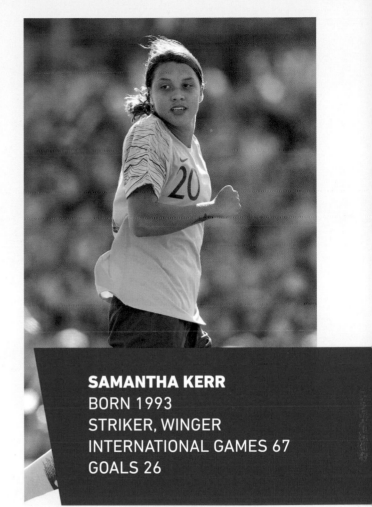

SAMANTHA KERR
BORN 1993
STRIKER, WINGER
INTERNATIONAL GAMES 67
GOALS 26

SOUTH KOREA

The South Koreans are, along with the Chinese, likely to follow in the footsteps of Japan and put up a strong fight against the US and the Europe in the race for the title. At the heart of the South Korean defense, Ji So-Yun's performance will play an important role. She is also the country's top goal scorer, of all time. So-Yun is one of Chelsea Women's most prominent players. Chelsea, with So-Yun onboard, won the Women's Super League in 2018, the top women's soccer league in England.

JI SO-YUN
BORN 1991
MIDFIELDER
INTERNATIONAL GAMES 109
GOALS 49

ALEX MORGAN

Alex Morgan will celebrate her 30th birthday five days before the 2019 World Cup final kicks off. If things go well for the WNT, there will be little time for birthday celebrations while the team plays in the semifinals determining who will proceed to fight for the top in Lyon. And that is precisely Morgan's goal. She will play an integral role in the team's success at the tournament, which will ultimately decide whether the US will get to defend its 2015 World Cup title. Morgan will be at the top of her game as the US's most dangerous and competent fighting machine. She is a natural-born sports star and would probably have excelled in any sport.

Morgan grew up in suburb of Los Angeles and it was a great fortune for American women's soccer that this sport became her passion. She received vast support from family and friends and immediately proved that she was poised for greatness. She was quick on her feet, strong and fearless at the goal, which soon landed her a position on the offense. She immediately began racking up goals. People often forget that she is just as good at setting up her teammates with countless assists, and always the target of the defense, which allows them all an opportunity to score.

Morgan is brimming with seemingly limitless energy, and when she is not scoring or making an assist. She writes soccer books for kids or works on a variety of other projects. She is one of the most visible professional athletes in the States and has contributed significantly to expanding the popularity of the sport, especially by advocating soccer to young girls across the country.

With an Olympic gold medal and World Cup title beneath her belt, it the clear that she remains a highly valuable asset for the 2019 World Cup. In recent years, Morgan has played with Portland Thorns and Orlando Pride. She then traveled to France in 2017 and joined Olympique Lyonnais for a time, Europe's strongest women's soccer team. There Morgan's strength was fully unleashed, with 12 goals in 16 games, and she was head and shoulders above the rest even among the world's best.

American soccer fans can rest assured that Morgan will put 110% into defending the title, and bringing home the desired cup. That will be a birthday celebration to remember.

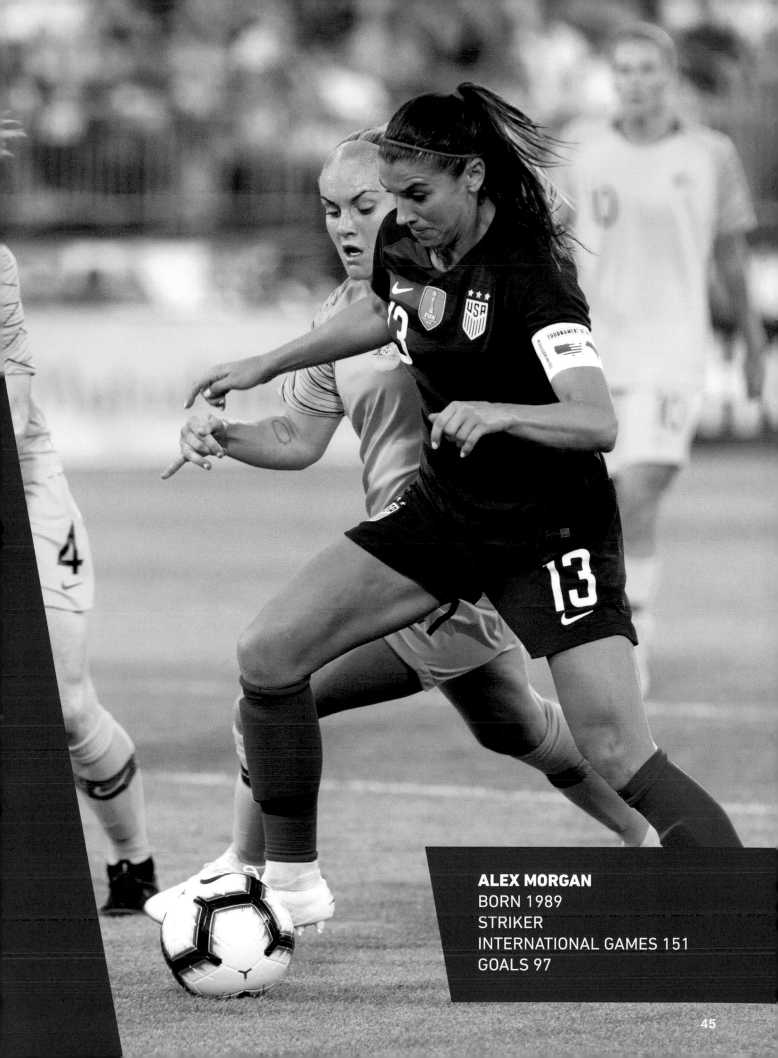

ALEX MORGAN
BORN 1989
STRIKER
INTERNATIONAL GAMES 151
GOALS 97

MEGAN RAPINOE

The World Cup tournament in France could be Megan Rapinoe's last, and she will undoubtedly fight hard for her team and title.

She has never lacked spirit, whether on the field or elsewhere, and found an outlet for her ambition soccer early on. Rapinoe hails from Redding in Northern California where she competed in both track and field and basketball before deciding to focus her efforts into soccer with her twin sister. Rapinoe's skills grew and she played her first international game at the age of 21, but she then suffered a devastating injury which for a time seemed career-threatening.

Rapinoe was absent from international games the next two years and missed the 2007 World Cup as well as the 2008 Summer Olympics in Beijing. In an interview, Rapinoe addressed the many lessons learned from struggling with her injury: "Before, everything was going how it was supposed to be and I wasn't really appreciative of what I was doing and what it took to be there. The injury grounded me in a lot of different ways. The rehab process makes you stronger on all fronts, mentally and physically. I feel stronger and a better person for it. I would never wish it on anyone, but I don't wish I could take it back."

Her words are emblematic of the determination and professionalism that characterize Rapinoe. She returned to play as a lightning-fast winger, and sometimes playmaker, and totally fearless. She became pillar of the 2011 World Cup team, scoring one goal and assisting three.

Her performance was even more outstanding during the Summer Olympics in London the following year. She scored three goals, two of which were in a hair-raising game against Canada, in the semifinals. She also achieved the rare feat of scoring straight from a corner kick.

At the 2015 World Cup, Rapinoe again made two goals in the WNT's first game against Australia, where the US won 3–1. She was then a powerful part of the team that clinched the title. Rapinoe is hard as nails, a natural born fighter, and her precision passes and shots will play a significant role for the US team at the 2019 World Cup in France.

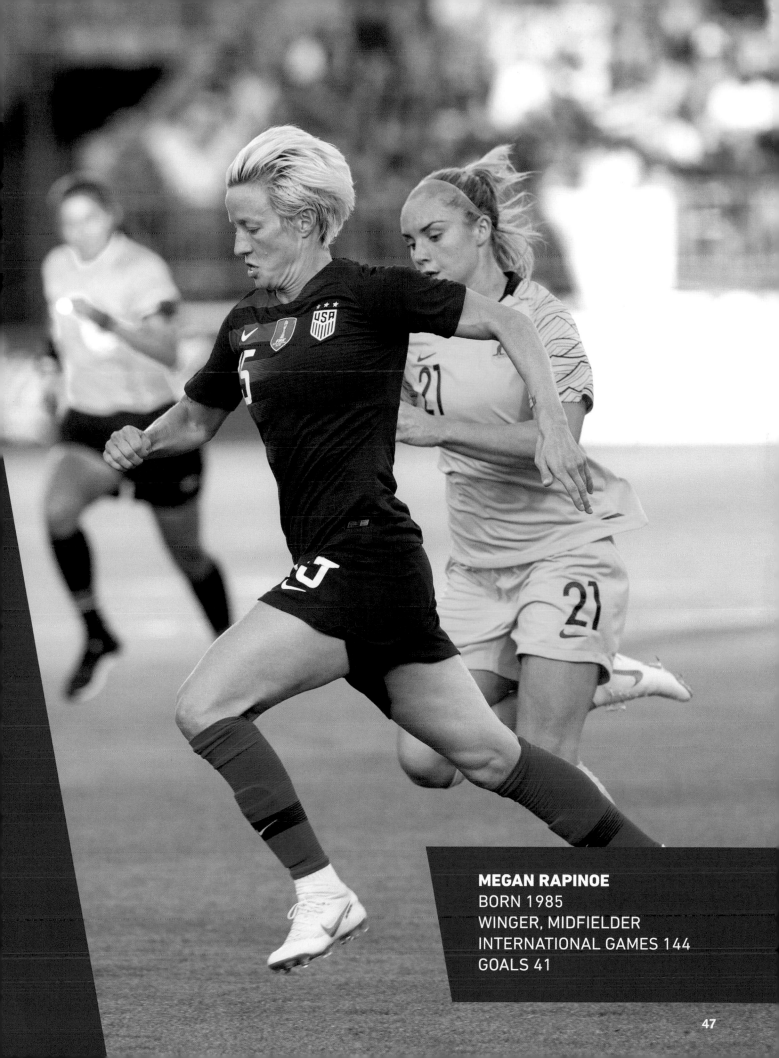

MEGAN RAPINOE
BORN 1985
WINGER, MIDFIELDER
INTERNATIONAL GAMES 144
GOALS 41

CARLI LLOYD

Aggressive midfielder Carli Lloyd had already earned a place in the history of American soccer before the 2015 World Cup. The US met Brazil in the final of the 2008 Summer Olympics in Beijing, but none of the forwards from either side could manage to get the ball into the net even as the game dragged into overtime. Then Lloyd took matters into her own hands and scored a glorious winning goal with a soaring long shot all the way from the halfway line, thereby taking the gold for the US. Four years later, Lloyd joined the national team in the Summer Olympics final in London, where the US squared off with Japan. In the 8th minute, Lloyd confidently fired the ball into the the net after a precision assist from Morgan. Japan went for an equalizer, but in the 54th minute Lloyd took the ball at great speed and launched a phenomenal long-range shot, scoring a second goal for the US. The US won the game 2–1 to defend their Olympic gold. Yet even this performance could not prepare fans for what would become Lloyd's superlative career achievement and a significant moment in the history of the World Cup to boot. Lloyd got a hat trick the 16th minute of the 2015 World Cup final, bringing yet another top title to the US. Lloyd will celebrate her 37th birthday around the end of the 2019 tournament, but she has really proven she still harbors the power and unquenchable fighting spirit required to make a difference at the highest levels.

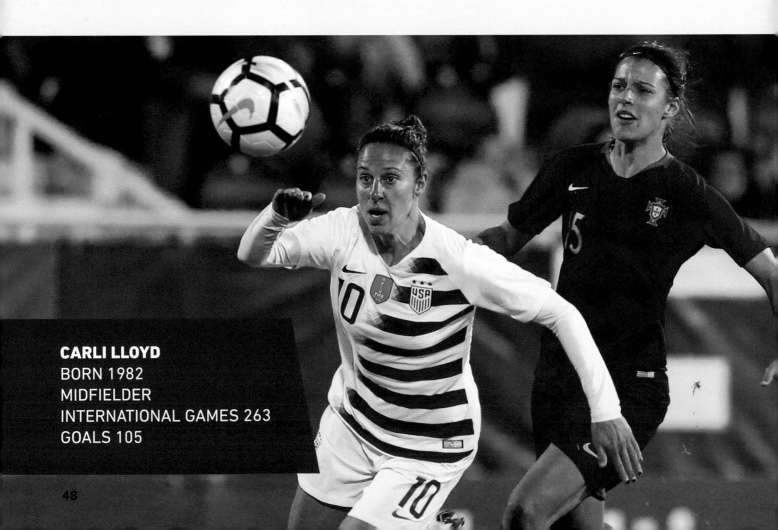

CARLI LLOYD
BORN 1982
MIDFIELDER
INTERNATIONAL GAMES 263
GOALS 105

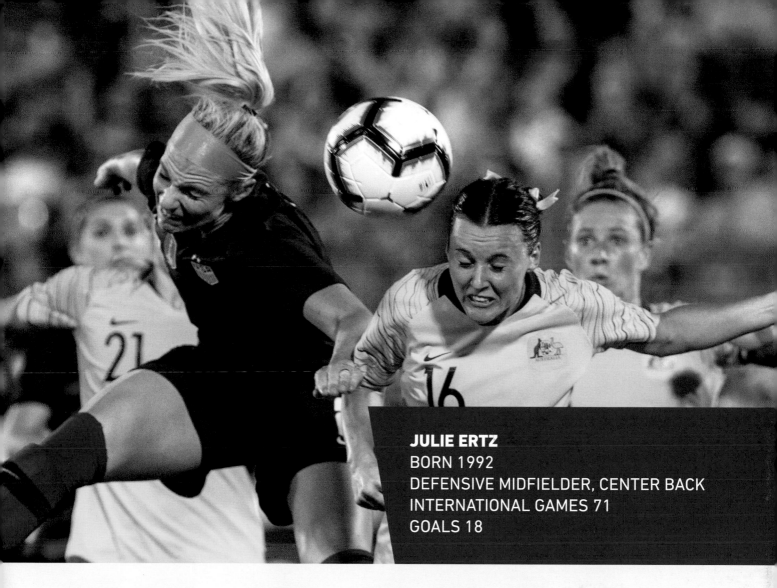

JULIE ERTZ
BORN 1992
DEFENSIVE MIDFIELDER, CENTER BACK
INTERNATIONAL GAMES 71
GOALS 18

JULIE ERTZ

Julie Johnston Ertz began her career with the WNT as a hard-tackling and unyielding center back. She's moved a little upfield in the last few years and now counts as a full-fledged defensive midfielder. Her role is to both break down the opponents' offense and get the ball as quickly as possible to the strongest forwards on her team. Asked about her many positions on the field, Ertz has said that she has "always valued the importance of being versatile. I've known it from club youth days, from college to [the WNT]. At the end of the day you want to do everything you can for your teammates and your team and what they ask of you . . . Obviously, I'm more comfortable being a center back, I've done it now for five years." She added that her position was demanding, with high expectations for quick tackles and equally speedy passes, but her love of the challenge is what essentially matters: "I like to win headers and be aggressive. Those are fun things for me to do. As a defensive mid, it is a lot more running and I've learned that you have to increase your speed of play in the center at this level, but I enjoy it."

BECKY SAUERBRUNN

At the time of writing, Becky Sauerbrunn has played almost 150 games for the US women's national team without scoring a single goal. Fortunately, scoring goals is not her job, and no one can doubt that despite this lack she is one of the most important players on the team. Sauerbrunn stands in a long distinguished line of powerful center backs that are no less paramount in the WNT's successes than the goal-scoring forwards. It is worth mentioning Carla Overbeck and Christie Rampone (now Pearce) in this context. Sauerbrunn was born in St. Louis and has played with teams across the whole United States. Wherever she lands, the opponent's goals drop off because of her seemingly infinite energy and equally expansive cunning. It came as no surprise when she was selected one of four captains for the US team, along with Alex Morgan, Carli Lloyd, and Megan Rapinoe.

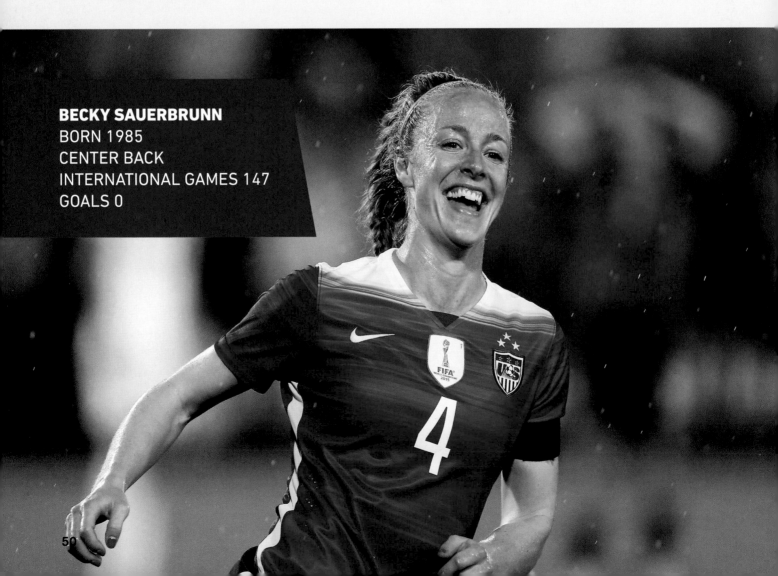

BECKY SAUERBRUNN
BORN 1985
CENTER BACK
INTERNATIONAL GAMES 147
GOALS 0

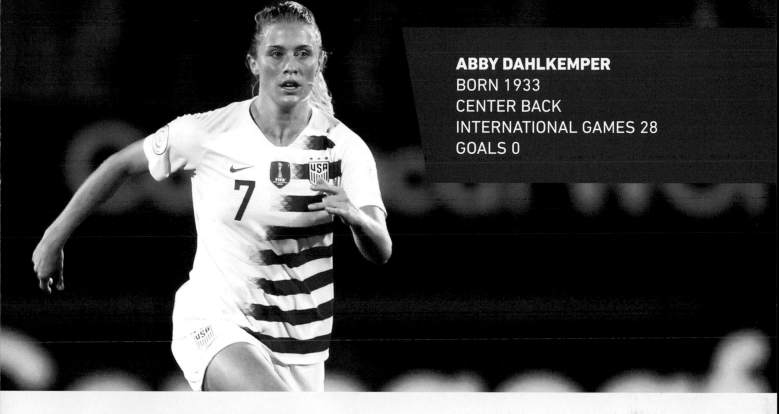

ABBY DAHLKEMPER

Abby Dahlkemper is nothing if not a fighter. She was born in Pennsylvania but grew up in California, and became a prominent center back early on. She played with all the US junior national teams but was never allowed to properly shine due to the tightly organized and carefully selected defensive lineup. Her chance came in a friendly game against Switzerland in 2016, but she was unfortunate enough to get a sepsis infection which required surgery and lengthy medical treatment. Commenting on the illness in an interview with espn.com, Dahlkemper said, "It was that time away that made me really want to get back on the field . . . It made me realize how much I love and cherish the game and playing. Everything happens for a reason. That

was a hard time, but it was an important time because I was able to build some resilience and realize how badly I wanted to achieve some goals of mine."

Dahlkemper fully recovered and returned to the team even more vigorous than before. In 2018, she played the most games of all the WNT and was on her path to become the backbone of the sturdy US defense, at the side of Julie Ertz and Becky Sauerbrunn.

Jill Ellis praised Dahlkemper's "distribution and her quality of delivery," also calling her "a natural playmaker from the back." The heart of the matter is, Ellis added, that you've "got to be brave to be in the back."

ALYSSA NAEHER

It was an epic leap for Alyssa Naeher to step into the shoes of Hope Solo and replace her in the goal. With her imposing presence Solo was the true leader of the defense. Yet Naeher stayed coolheaded, not a trace of fear in her expression, and sturdy as a goalkeeper should be when she accepted the position. She rarely breaks under pressure and will resiliently stand guard for years to come. She is from Bridgeport, Connecticut, and has played with various teams in the United States but she also played with the steadfast German team Turbine Potsdamfor two years. Naeher has a twin sister named Amanda, who also played soccer in college and was a prolific goal scorer. Naeher gleefully explained on the US soccer website why she had decided to become a goalkeeper: Her father was a high school soccer coach and recruited the twins as ball girls. A reward for their diligence was a trip to the local sports store. Both sisters were allowed choose one object, but Naeher "wanted something different," explaining that she liked the idea that she "could wear a different shirt from everyone else . . . I remember picking out my first gloves, blue and white—I still have them."

ALYSSA NAEHER
BORN 1988
GOALKEEPER
INTERNATIONAL GAMES 37

CRYSTAL DUNN

Crystal Dunn is a versatile player with many positions under her belt, but her eyes are always also fastened on the goal. She has played forward for the offense but recently is very engaged in the role of winger. Still, her attacking days are far from over. Addressing her versatility on the field, Dunn said she wants "to be remembered as Crystal Dunn a good soccer player. I want to be remembered as Crystal Dunn a good teammate, someone that was there for me, someone that was encouraging."

CRYSTAL DUNN
BORN 1992
RIGHT BACK, WINGER
INTERNATIONAL GAMES 74
GOALS 24

KELLEY O'HARA

Kelley O'Hara began her soccer careers as a spirited forward. She was later transferred to left winger, and then once again moved, this time to left back. And there she properly came into her own. She dashes from one spot to the next, tackles, and then shoots effortless passes that send the ball dancing into the center of the oppenent's goal area.

KELLEY O'HARA
BORN 1988
LEFT BACK, WINGER
INTERNATIONAL GAMES 112
GOALS 2

LINDSEY HORAN

For a WNT player, Lindsey Horan's climb to the top has taken a somewhat unusual path. She was born in Golden, Colorado, and attracted attention at a young age for her toughness and tenacity as a forward. And that's the position she played with junior WNT teams where she racked up goals. At only 18, Horan went to France to join one of Europe's most powerful teams, Paris Saint-Germain. There she played offense, alongside one of France's most dangerous forwards, Marie-Laure Delie. Over a period of four years Horan played in 76 games and scored 54 goals. She has a multifaceted style and a special knack for scoring headers, whether from assists or corners. Despite her successes with PSG, Horan's European excursion stood in the way of her desire to serve on the US national team, so she returned home. She moved to the center of the field when she returned to the Portland Thorns but nevertheless maintained her goal scoring stride. She was selected Most Valuable Player for the National Women's Soccer League in 2018. And she has had a permanent place at the center ever since. Horan is still developing as a player, but her promise will become a great asset for the WNT in the years to come.

LINDSEY HORAN
BORN 1994
STRIKER, ATTACKING MIDFIELDER
INTERNATIONAL GAMES 61
GOALS 7

ROSE LAVELLE
BORN 1995
MIDFIELDER
INTERNATIONAL GAMES 18
GOALS 6

ROSE LAVELLE

Following the 2015 win, the WNT went on a trip across the United States on a so-called Victory Tour. The tour recruited a number of girls who were seen to have a future with the WNT. Among them was the 20-year-old midfielder Rose Lavelle from the Buckeye State. In 2014, Lavelle had been awarded the Golden Ball as top player of the CONCACAF Women's Under-20 Championship. She had also proven to be proficient both at scoring and assisting over three seasons in Wisconsin. Lavelle did not join the WNT until March 2017, but coach Ellis put great faith in her. And Lavelle immediately set out to show that she belonged on the team. During the 2018 CONCACAF Women's Championship, Lavelle had finally found her place in the team, often leaving veteran Morgan Brian on the bench. Lavelle scored three goals, the first in a game where the US beat Canada 2–0 in the final. The goal arrived only a minute into the game, and this is only the beginning.

TOBIN HEATH

According to soccer lingo, the term "Brazilian" is used to describe technical abilities, dribbling skills, individual virtuosity, and a particular knack for offense. That fact that Tobin Heath is often dubbed "the Brazilian" of the WNT is a clear sign of her impeccable talents. An ever-agile midfielder, Heath comes from Basking Ridge in New Jersey. She has traveled widely over her soccer career but also been challenged by difficult injuries. However, when Heath is at her best, she dazzles fans with her vigor and agility. She is now at the height of her career and will likely be instrumental in the WNT's climb to the top in France.

TOBIN HEATH
BORN 1988
WINGER
INTERNATIONAL GAMES 142
GOALS 25

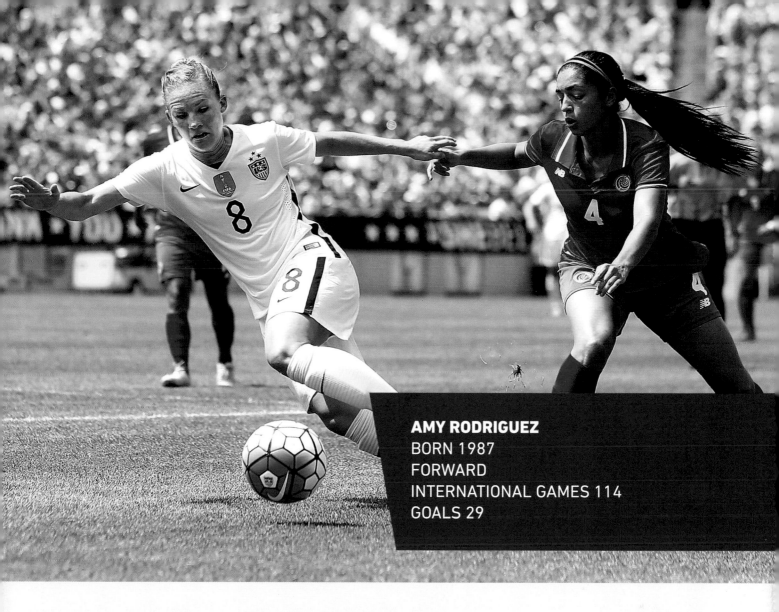

AMY RODRIGUEZ
BORN 1987
FORWARD
INTERNATIONAL GAMES 114
GOALS 29

AMY RODRIGUEZ

Amy Rodriguez is a tough and sharp-shooting attacking player who never checks out. A native of Lake Forest, California, Rodriguez stands out among most top women players in that she had two children while still at the high point of her career. Most players put their child-rearing on hold until their career begins to slow down, but through relentless determination, Rodriguez was back in top shape in no time and picked up the game right where she left off. However, a severe injury in 2017 put her career on pause once again, and she was forced to leave soccer for over a year. She has now recovered and is eager to join her teammates at the 2019 World Cup. US head coach Jill Ellis spoke about Rodriguez's resilience on the WNT website, musing on how remarkable her return was, adding "I know the work she's put into it." Ellis went on to underscore her awe of the forward, with "two young boys, it's exceptional."

Her commitment is fantastic. She still has the same qualities and she's just a great human being," coach Ellis concluded.

CHRISTEN PRESS

Christen Press is a ferociously strong but at the same time brisk goal scorer from Los Angeles. She was 25 years old when she was first chosen for the WNT, but since then she has never looked back and uses every opportunity to score. Her example is a great reminder of the value of never giving up on your hopes and dreams for success. Even though she often joined games as a substitute, in five years Press had built up a track record of over 100 international games with a goal in almost every other one.

CHRISTEN PRESS
BORN 1988
STRIKER
INTERNATIONAL GAMES 106
GOALS 46

MALLORY PUGH

Mallory Pugh is one the most promising forwards to emerge in American soccer in recent years. She hails from Colorado and was only 18 when she played her first international game. When she scored a goal during the Summer Olympics in Rio de Janeiro, she became the youngest player ever to do so for the United States at the Olympics.

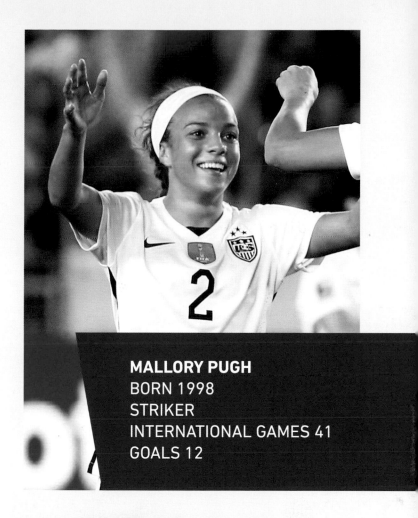

MALLORY PUGH
BORN 1998
STRIKER
INTERNATIONAL GAMES 41
GOALS 12

MORGAN BRIAN

At the age of 22, Morgan Brian was the youngest player on the US team that won the 2015 World Cup in Canada. She played in six games, starting in four of them, and she provided an assist for the last goal of the final scored by Tobin Heath. Her passing skills and sharp assists might prove vital in France in 2019.

MORGAN BRIAN
BORN 1993
MIDFIELDER
INTERNATIONAL GAMES 81
GOALS 6

THE COACH

Jill Ellis's journey to become coach of a world championship soccer team is rather unusual. She was born in the nerve center of soccer itself, England, where she ran track and field. But soccer remained mostly a no-go for her given its reputation in the 1980s as "unfeminine," though occasionally random boys would allow her to join in informal games here and there, when it suited them. At the age of 15, she moved to the United States where her father, an ex-marine, was offered a job as a soccer coach. Soccer was at the time an undeveloped and rather unpopular sport in the US, so Ellis took the easy opportunity to play the sport without the hurdles she had faced back home. Soccer was not her only interest, nor sports in general. At university she was an English literature major and claims she still loves to curl up on the couch with a good novel. But soccer began to demand more time out of her schedule. She played with her university team but found herself drawn to coaching and eventually began working with the UCLA soccer team. She served as UCLA coach for 11 successful years, gravitating gradually to the WNT and coaching junior teams for a time. Then 2014 then proved a fateful year. The WNT coach at the time performed poorly and was eventually fired. He had been tasked with winning the World Cup title in Canada the following year, but now the WNT was facing a potential disaster. Ellis was asked to intervene, and she was fully aware that the expectation was no less than the elusive Cup itself, which the US had not seen since 1999. Despite the pressure, she began her World Cup project with the calm and composure that would come to define her coaching style. Ellis's qualities were contagious and spread throughout the WNT, injecting the players with such confidence that they sailed into the tournament and breezily defeated one team after the other, finally once again embracing the much-desired cup.

With Ellis at the helm, the WNT plays with straight-edged precision and grace, and a take-no-prisoners attitude. During the 2016 Summer Olympics in Moscow, the US failed to defend their 2004, 2008, and 2012 titles, but the team had no problems winning the 2018 CONCACAF Women's Champions. Alex Morgan was the top goal scorer, with seven goals in four games, though Julie Ertz was chosen the tournament's best player. The team is therefore in excellent shape for the coming World Cup, and in Ellis's safe hands, though as usual and true to her character she refrains from making any grand statements about possible victories.

MATCH SCHEDULE

GROUP A | SCORE

JUNE 7, 4:00 PM			PARIS
FRANCE			**SOUTH KOREA**
JUNE 8, 4:00 PM			REIMS
NORWAY			**NIGERIA**
JUNE 12, 11:00 AM			GRENOBLE
NIGERIA			**SOUTH KOREA**
JUNE 12, 4:00 PM			NICE
FRANCE			**NORWAY**
JUNE 17, 4:00 PM			RENNES
NIGERIA			**FRANCE**
JUNE 17, 4:00 PM			REIMS
SOUTH KOREA			**NORWAY**

TEAM	P	W	D	L	F	A	PTS

GROUP B | SCORE

JUNE 8, 10:00 AM			RENNES
GERMANY			**CHINA PR**
JUNE 8, 1:00 PM			LE HAVRE
SPAIN			**SOUTH AFRICA**
JUNE 12, 1:00 PM			VALENCIENNES
GERMANY			**SPAIN**
JUNE 13, 4:00 PM			PARIS
SOUTH AFRICA			**CHINA PR**
JUNE 17, 1:00 PM			MONTPELLIER
SOUTH AFRICA			**GERMANY**
JUNE 17, 1:00 PM			LE HAVRE
CHINA PR			**SPAIN**

TEAM	P	W	D	L	F	A	PTS

GROUP C | SCORE

JUNE 9, 8:00 AM			VALENCIENNES
AUSTRALIA			**ITALY**
JUNE 9, 10:30 AM			GRENOBLE
BRAZIL			**JAMAICA**
JUNE 13, 1:00 PM			MONTPELLIER
AUSTRALIA			**BRAZIL**
JUNE 14, 1:00 PM			REIMS
JAMAICA			**ITALY**
JUNE 18, 4:00 PM			GRENOBLE
JAMAICA			**AUSTRALIA**
JUNE 18, 4:00 PM			VALENCIENNES
ITALY			**BRAZIL**

TEAM	P	W	D	L	F	A	PTS

GROUP D | SCORE

JUNE 9, 1:00 PM			NICE
ENGLAND			**SCOTLAND**
JUNE 10, 1:00 PM			PARIS
ARGENTINA			**JAPAN**
JUNE 14, 10:00 AM			RENNES
JAPAN			**SCOTLAND**
JUNE 14, 4:00 PM			LE HAVRE
ENGLAND			**ARGENTINA**
JUNE 19, 4:00 PM			NICE
JAPAN			**ENGLAND**
JUNE 19, 4:00 PM			PARIS
SCOTLAND			**ARGENTINA**

TEAM	P	W	D	L	F	A	PTS

GROUP E | SCORE

JUNE 10, 4:00 PM			MONTPELLIER
CANADA			**CAMEROON**
JUNE 11, 10:00 AM			LE HAVRE
NEW ZEALAND			**NETHERLANDS**
JUNE 15, 10:00 AM			VALENCIENNES
NETHERLANDS			**CAMEROON**
JUNE 15, 4:00 PM			GRENOBLE
CANADA			**NEW ZEALAND**
JUNE 20, 1:00 PM			REIMS
NETHERLANDS			**CANADA**
JUNE 20, 1:00 PM			MONTPELLIER
CAMEROON			**NEW ZEALAND**

TEAM	P	W	D	L	F	A	PTS

GROUP F | SCORE

JUNE 11, 1:00 PM			RENNES
CHILE			**SWEDEN**
JUNE 11, 4:00 PM			REIMS
UNITED STATES			**THAILAND**
JUNE 16, 10:00 AM			NICE
SWEDEN			**THAILAND**
JUNE 16, 1:00 PM			PARIS
UNITED STATES			**CHILE**
JUNE 20, 4:00 PM			LE HAVRE
SWEDEN			**UNITED STATES**
JUNE 20, 4:00 PM			RENNES
THAILAND			**CHILE**

TEAM	P	W	D	L	F	A	PTS

ALL MATCHES ARE LISTED IN EASTERN STANDARD TIME